How Now, Brown Cow?

How
now,
brown
cow?
How's it going?
Just stopped by—
heard you lowing. . . .
Lovely view.
Lovely weather.

Good to have
this moo
together.

The Cow

You come across her standing there
as common as a box. As square.
Her lower jaw revolves the cud;
her hooves stand foursquare in the mud.
Come closer. View with mild surprise
the gentle softness of her eyes.

The Cow's Complaint

How unkind to keep me here
When, over there, the grass is greener.
Tender blades—so far, so near—
How unkind to keep me here!
Through this fence they make me peer
At sweeter stems; what could be meaner?
How unkind to keep me here
When, over there, the grass is greener.

Milking

Blowing
clouds of white breath
into the icy morning
he leans his forehead into her
warm side

his hands
moving, sending
the steaming streams ringing
against the side of the metal
milk pail

as her
jaws move, chewing
the good grain, blowing clouds
of warm breath into the melting
morning.

Clever Cows

The clever cows
in single file
walk up the hill
and stop awhile.

Then, black and brindle,
red and brown,
    they
       make
         a
           line
             and
              walk
                back
                  down.

Consider Cow

Consider cow
which rhymes
with bough
but not
with rough.
That's clear
enough.

Remember moo
will rhyme
with through
but not
with trough
or though
or tough.

You've got
it now:
There's dough
and bough
and cough
and through
and mough . . .
er, moo.

The Bull

Do they watch me trot to the top of the hill,
the cows who are milling and mooing?
      I bellow and blow and paw the ground
      and make a sort of a snorting sound
      and toss my terrible horns around—
(The cows—have they stopped their chewing?)

I'm striking a pose; I'm standing still
as a statue here on the top of the hill.
      I flick my tail, as I stately stand,
      at a fool of a fly who has dared to land
      on the royal rump of a bull so grand—
(Are they watching whatever I'm doing?)

Taradiddle

She landed hard,
they say,
and afterward was slightly lame.
For several days
the curious came to stare,
and many hoped
that she would dare
to try the trick again.
They went away dissatisfied.
She never tried
to jump again,
but gazed for hours at the moon.
They never found the dish and spoon.

Drivin' the Cows

Drivin' the cows to Wyomin'
Two, three head at a crack,
Gas up the Ford
Git along! All aboard!
Up to Wyomin' and back.

Buttercup settin' beside me
Daisy and Blanche behind,
All squeezed in—sardines in a tin—
Watchin' the road unwind.

Headin' on down the highway
Fast as the law allows,
All the livelong day
Yippee-i-ki-ay!
Gonna be drivin' these cows.

Moo

No matter the time,
the place, or season,
with no excuse,
for no known reason,
in the middle of a meadow
a cow says "Moo!"
Then all
the other cows
say it, too.

What does
moo mean,
anyway?
What,
exactly,
are they trying to say?

No matter what else
they're thinking of doing,
if they're cows
they're probably
thinking of mooing.

A Cow Looks Down the Highway

Poor silly things
    they never see
a thistle
    or a bumblebee;
closed up inside
    their shiny shells
they cannot know
    how clover smells.
I wonder why
    they hurry so.
Why do they think
    they have to go
so fast—as if
    the grass won't last
until tomorrow?

April 1

The sun
came up wearing
a mustache, starlings stood
on their heads along telephone
wires,

all the
sweet brown cows gave
chocolate milk, and a
frisky white one gave vanilla
milk shakes.

Cows Live Here

Cows live here
    you must
    step over
meadow muffins
    in the
    clover
pasture paddies
    cowpies
    buns
drying, fly-ing
    in the
    sun
watch-your-steppers
    don't-look-ups

and every spring a
    thousand
    thousand
    buttercups.

Shelter

Her hooves
sinking into
the snow-soaked meadow, she
moves heavily toward sheltering
aspen. . . .

Among
shivering leaves
she waits, smelling the wind,
her head turned slightly as if she
listens. . . .

At dawn
a newborn calf
follows closely at her
side, his small hooves denting the wet
prairie.

Cows Coming Home

Just here
part the grass
find the path
worn smooth
as stone
worn by hooves
of cows coming home
cows coming home
at sundown.

Wait for dusk
you can
just hear
cowbells
you can just see
shadows
cows coming home
cows coming home
at sundown.

Requests for permission to make copies of any part of the work
should be mailed to: Permissions Department, Harcourt Brace & Company,
6277 Sea Harbor Drive, Orlando, Florida 32887-6777.

Library of Congress Cataloging-in-Publication Data
Schertle, Alice.
How now, brown cow?/poems by Alice Schertle; paintings by
Amanda Schaffer.—1st ed.
p.   cm.
"Browndeer Press."
ISBN 0-15-276648-0
1. Cows—Poetry. I. Title
PS3569.C48435H68   1994
811'.54—dc20   93-24052

First edition
A B C D E

The paintings in this book were done in oils on canvas.
The display type was set in Recklman Hand Tooled.
The text type was set in Goudy Village
by Thompson Type, San Diego, California.
Color separations by Bright Arts, Ltd., Singapore
Printed and bound by Tien Wah Press, Singapore
This book was printed with soya-based inks on Leykam recycled paper,
which contains more than 20 percent postconsumer waste and has
a total recycled content of at least 50 percent.
Production supervision by
Warren Wallerstein and David Hough
Designed by Lisa Peters

For Spencer

—Alice Schertle

*To my father Albert and mother Lillian,
and to family and friends for their generous support and
encouragement, which makes anything seem possible.*

—Amanda Schaffer